Flying Models

Mary Jean McNeil

Illustrated by Colin King
Designed by John Jamieson

Models designed by Derek Beck
Educational Adviser: Frank Blackwell

D0479652

Contents

About Flying Models

The aeroplanes in this book are all made from paper and card. If you want to colour them, use Magic Marker, not paints. For the planes which need gluing, use quick-drying, powerful glue such as UHU or Bostik 1.

⊙ Boxes with this sign give you special tips for making the models.

🚩 Boxes with this sign give you special tips for flying the models.

We have used the words 'paper' and 'card' and 'thick card' in this book.

Paper means any normal writing paper, not newspaper.

Card means any thin card about the thickness of a postcard, although actual postcards will be too small. You may use old card folders. If you have to buy them, ask at a stationer for a document folder or square cut folder.

Thick card means really stiff strong card such as the card you find on the back of some writing pads and calendars.

First published in 1975

Usborne Publishing Ltd
20 Garrick Street
London WC2E 9BJ

© **Usborne Publishing Ltd 1975**

The name Usborne and the device 🪂 are Trade Marks of Usborne Publishing Ltd.

This abridged edition contains the best projects from the original 48-page version.

Made and printed in Great Britain by Purnell and Sons (Book Production) Limited Paulton, Bristol

KH01 Prototype

The KH01 Prototype is a very easy plane to make. You can make it from a sheet of paper 21cm × 29cm. Ask for A4 paper. If you cannot make it fly properly, look at the Flying Boxes in the middle of this page. You can find out how to launch it on the next page.

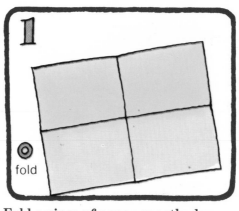

1 fold

Fold a piece of paper exactly down the middle. Unfold it. Fold it exactly down the middle in the other direction. These folds are your guide lines.

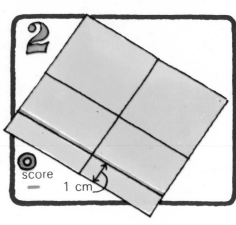

2 score — 1 cm

Score a line 1 cm from the long edge of the paper. Then fold the paper up along this line as shown.

The KH01 Prototype

If it Stalls

paper clip

Planes can fly badly in lots of different ways. Sometimes they stall. A stalling plane goes up and down and up and down like this. It stalls because its nose is not heavy enough. Put a paper clip on its front like this. Launch it. If it still stalls put on another one. Or try putting a bit of tape along the folded edge.

2

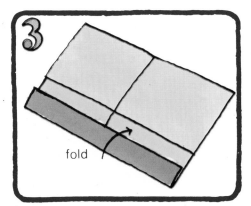

Fold the paper again and again until your folded edge reaches the middle guide line.

The last fold has to be really tight, so press your ruler down hard on the paper and run it along the edge.

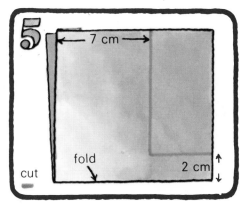

Fold the paper in half with the folded paper on the inside. Draw and cut out the aeroplane shape as shown.

If it Dives

Your plane may dive nose first to the ground. This may mean that the nose is too heavy. Or it may mean that the tail is not working properly. Make a small cut each side of the tail and bend the paper up as shown. Launch it again. If it still dives, bend the paper up a bit more. Keep doing this until the plane glides smoothly.

Aeroplanes

Aeroplanes have lots of different parts. Each part has its own special job.

Look at the aeroplane here and see where the parts are and what they do.

Folding Paper in Half

For paper aeroplanes, paper folds must be really accurate. The best way is to hold the edges together with your fingers while you smooth the fold down with your thumbs.

Scoring

Lay the paper on something hard and flat. Put your ruler along the line you want to score. Rule a line with a ball point pen. Press the pen down hard all the time.

The Free Flyer

The Free Flyer flies through the air in a very smooth, slow glide. You can make it from a sheet of paper 21cm × 29cm (A4 paper). On this page you will find out how to launch it properly and how to make it turn left and right. All flattish planes like the Free Flyer are launched in this way.

Follow boxes one to four for the KH01 Prototype. Then fold the paper in half with the folded edge on the outside. Draw and cut out the Free Flyer shape as shown.

Score a line 1 cm from the tips of the wings. Bend the top wing edge over the score line and bend the bottom one over in the opposite direction as shown.

The Free Flyer

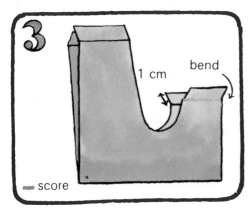

3

1 cm · bend

score

Fold the plane the other way. Score a line 1 cm from the tip of the tail as shown. Bend the tail tips over the score line in opposite directions to each other.

4

bend down

Bend the back wing edges down by running them between your thumb and fingers. This will curve the wing edge and the plane will fly better. It is called cambering.

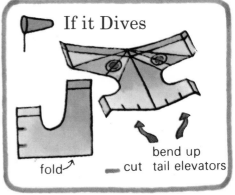

If it Dives

fold · cut · tail elevators · bend up

Fold the plane and make two snips in the tail as shown. Unfold the plane. Bend them up until the plane flies smoothly. These are called tail elevators.

Launching a Free Flyer

Put your fore-finger on top of the plane like this with your thumb and other fingers underneath. Point the plane in the direction you want it to go.

Move your hand forward at the speed you think it will fly at and just let it go. Do not jerk or push it forward. Just let it glide from your hand.

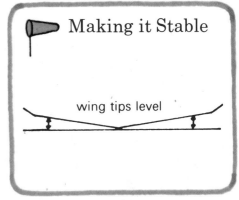

Making it Stable

wing tips level

An unstable plane will spin and somersault to the ground. Hold it up like this. Make sure that the wing tips are level. Push them up or down to make them level.

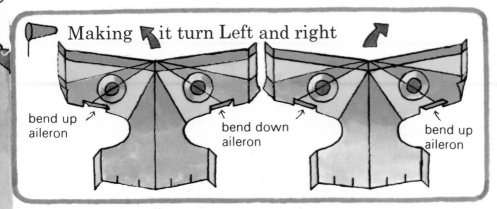

Making it turn Left and right

bend up aileron · bend down aileron · bend up aileron

If you want to, you can make the Free Flyer fly in different directions. Make two little cuts in the back of the wings as shown, to make ailerons.

To make it go left, bend the left aileron up and the right aileron down. To make it go right, bend the right aileron up and the left one down.

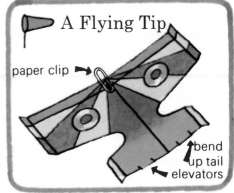

A Flying Tip

paper clip · bend up tail elevators

The Free Flyer will fly very well if you put a paper clip on its nose and bend the tail elevators up a bit.

5

Buffalo Mark 1 and 2

Buffalo Mk 1 and 2, with their big, heavy folded noses are very good at flying tricks. You can make them from a sheet of paper 21cm × 29cm. Ask for A4 paper. As they do not have keels you will have to launch them in the same way that you launched the Free Flyer.
See page 5

Buffalo Mark 1

1 Buffalo Mk 1

mark on both edges

— score

Fold the paper in half and put it along the line at the top of this page like this. Mark A on both edges of the paper and score a line as shown.

2

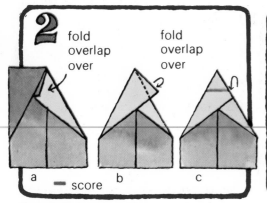

fold overlap over

fold overlap over

a — score   b   c

Open the paper. Fold one corner along the score line (a), fold the other corner over and fold back any paper that overlaps (b). Score across the top and fold it back (c).

3

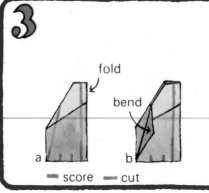

fold

bend

a   b

— score   — cut

Fold the paper in half like this. Score two more lines as shown (a). Bend the paper over both score lines and cut two snips in the bottom as shown (b).

4

bend tail elevators up

Open the paper out again so that it looks like this. You launch it this way up. Bend the tail elevators up if it dives or glides too steeply.

Buffalo Mark 2

1 Buffalo Mk 2

fold fold fold fold

a b c d

To make guide lines you will have to fold the paper four times, a, b, c, d, and unfold it four times. You unfold it after you have made each fold before you make the next.

2

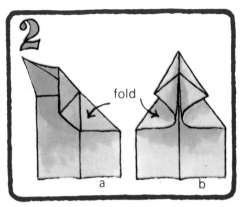

fold

a b

Open the paper out flat. Fold one side down like this (a). Then fold the other side down in the same way (b).

3

open out   press down

hold

a b

Hold the folds you have just made down with one hand. Open the top of the paper out with the other (a). Press the paper down as shown (b).

4

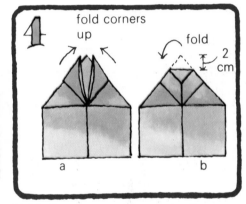

fold corners up

fold

2 cm

a b

Fold the two corners up to the point (a). Press them down. Fold 2 cm of the pointed nose down on to the dart as shown (b).

5

push corner into pocket

You will have made two pockets at the top of the paper. Push the remaining two corners into the pockets as shown.

6

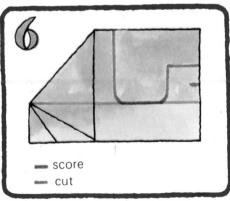

— score
— cut

Fold the paper in half and score a line as shown. Draw and cut out the aeroplane shape. Cut two tail elevator snips in the back.

7

Bend the paper over at the score line so that the plane looks like this. The middle should point downwards as shown. The dart is quite open. It has no keel.

The Air Scorpion

The Air Scorpion is a racing plane. It has swept-back wings and it flies very fast and straight.

You will need
THE PATTERN FOR ITS TAIL
  FIN ON PAGE 28
a sheet of paper 21cm × 29cm
a ball point pen for scoring
scissors
a ruler
sticky tape

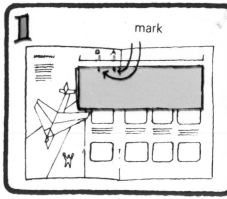

1

mark

Fold the paper in half like this. Put it along the line at the top of this page. Mark A and B on both edges of the paper.

5

third line   B   A   first line

fold back

1·25 cm   second line   1·25 cm

Fold the paper down the middle and fold the nose in. Draw three lines, one from A down to the fold, another across the bottom of the paper and the last from B as shown.

🚩 Launching it

Hold the plane by its keel. Point it down a bit and let it go gently.

The Air Scorpion

8

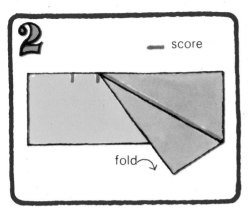

2 — score

Score a line from A to the top of the fold. Fold one of the corners over along this line as shown. Then fold the other corner back the other way.

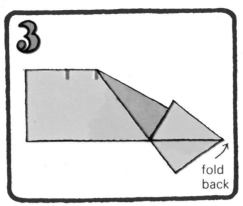

3

Fold both the corners back as shown.

4 tape

Open the paper out. It should look like this from the front (a). Turn it over and fold both the corners over tightly. Tape them down (b).

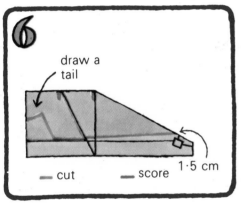

6 draw a tail — cut — score — 1·5 cm

Draw a tail shape and cut the plane out as shown. Score a line across the wings as shown. Score another across the tail.

7 bend wings and tail level — tape

Bend the tail and wings along the score line so that they are level. Keep the wings in place with tape and tape the front of the nose.

8 — cut — trace — fold — tape

Trace the tail fin pattern on to a folded piece of paper. Cut it out. Tape it inside the body of the plane, fold first, so that it sticks out a bit like this.

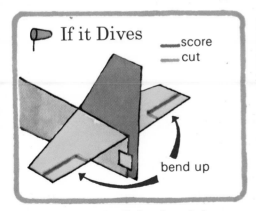

⚑ If it Dives — score — cut — bend up

You can stop it diving by giving it tail elevators. Make a cut each side of the tail fin as shown. Bend the tail elevators up a little. (see page 5).

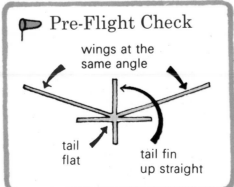

⚑ Pre-Flight Check

wings at the same angle

tail flat

tail fin up straight

Hold your plane up and see if it looks like this. The wings must be at the same angle. The tail should be flat and the tail fin should point straight up.

◎ Making a Tracing

draw   scribble   draw

Draw the outline on tracing paper. Turn it over and scribble over the outline with a pencil. Put the tracing, right side up, on paper and draw round the outline again.

The Range Moth

You will need
THE PATTERN FROM
    PAGE 28
a big sheet of paper at least
    30cm × 44cm
tracing paper and a pencil
a ball point pen cap, bits of
    card or plasticine
scissors, sticky tape and glue
see page 9 on making a tracing

If you want to, you can make a
parachute as well.
You will need
some polythene 20cm × 20cm
a big paper clip
scissors and thread

Trace the pattern on to a folded
piece of paper. Remember to trace
the score line as well. Cut the
plane out, but do not cut along
the fold.

Put a ruler exactly on to the score
lines. Score one line across the
wing, score another line across the
tail as shown.

Bend the wings and tail down along
the score lines as shown.

Trace the tail fin on to a folded
piece of paper. Cut it out, but not
along the fold. Tape the tail fin,
fold first into the inside back of the
plane as shown.

Cut out a piece of paper 6 cm ×
6 cm (a). Fold it in half (b). Open it
out and draw two guide lines 1 cm
from the fold as shown (c).

Glue the plane down on to this
piece of paper as shown. The wings
are following the guide lines you
drew on the piece of paper. Trim
any paper that overlaps.

Tape the plastic cap of a felt or
ball point pen into the nose. If
you want to, you can cut out small
strips of card and glue them into
the nose instead.

Cut out a narrow strip of paper
11 cm long. Fold it in half. Hold it
under the plane. Tape it to each
side of the wings so that the wings
tilt up at the same angle.

The Range Moth

A Parachute

1 Making a Parachute

tie
tie
tie
tie
big
paper
clip →

Cut some thread into four equal
lengths about 18 cm long. Tie each
thread to a corner of a square bit
of polythene. Tie the other ends
of the threads to a big paper clip.

2

← tiny cut

Launch the parachute from
somewhere nice and high. If it
sways too much on its way down,
make a tiny cut in the middle
as shown.

Pre-Flight Check

wings at
this angle

tail fin
straight

tail flat

The plane should look like this if
you hold it up in front of you.
The tail fin must point straight
up with the tail pieces flat. Wings
must be at an angle.

If it Stalls

push in
plasticine

Weight the top of the nose with
plasticine until the plane glides
smoothly. Then push the same
plasticine into the pen cap with a
pencil as shown.

If it Dives

bend up

Try giving it elevators on the
tail (see page 5) and bend them
up, as shown.

The Moon Bug

You will find that the Moon Bug is a very easy aeroplane to make. See page 9 on making a tracing.

You will need
THE MOON BUG PATTERN
  ON PAGE 28
a sheet of paper 21cm × 29cm
tracing paper and a pencil
scissors and sticky tape
a ruler
a ball point pen for scoring

Fold the paper and trace the plane and tail pattern on to it. Cut it out, but do not cut along the fold. Trace the lines on the wings and tail. Score the tail as shown.

To make the nose of this aeroplane, you will have to make guide lines. Start with the paper opened out (a). Then, fold one of the corners over as shown (b).

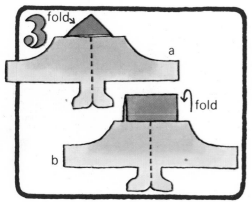

Fold the other corner over (a). Open the paper out and make a third fold (b) like this. Open the paper out for the last time and you have your guide lines.

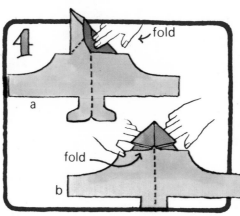

Make a fold like this on one side of the paper (a). Hold this fold down and fold the other side down in the same way (b).

Hold the paper folds in place with one hand and with the other open the paper above them out (a). Then press all the paper down (b).

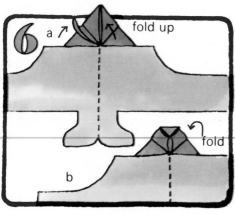

Fold the two bottom corners up as shown (a). Then fold the pointed end down (b).

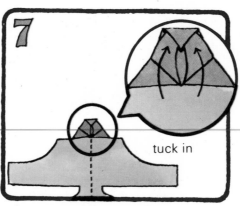

When you folded the pointed end down, you made little pockets at the top of the paper. Tuck the two free corners right into the pockets as shown.

Fold the paper in half. Put your ruler along the top of the fuselage and score a line across the wings.

9

bend wings over score line

Bend the wings back along the score line so that they are level.

10

tape

tape

tape

Tape the plane together at the nose and across the top of the wings. Tape the tail fin together as shown.

11

←tape wing tip on to line

tape wing tip on to line →

Curl the wing tips over and tape them on to the wings at the traced lines as shown.

12

tape on tail

bend

Bend the tail along its score lines and tape it under the tail fin so that the back of the plane looks like this.

Moon Bugs

13

The Drinking Straw Glider

The Drinking Straw Glider has a special kind of curved wing. It is called a cambered wing. The camber gives the plane a little more lift. See page 9 on making a tracing

You will need
THE PATTERN FROM PAGE 29
a sheet of paper for the wings and tail
card from a document folder
2 drinking straws
tracing paper and a pencil
scissors and a ruler
plasticine or silver foil
strong glue and sticky tape

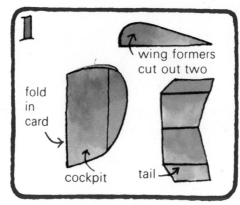

Trace and cut out a card cockpit, two card wing formers and a paper tail. Remember to trace all the lines on the patterns.

Cut out a paper wing as shown (a). Fold the paper in half and draw a line 1·5 cm from the fold (b). Open the wings out and cut a notch into the fold as shown (c).

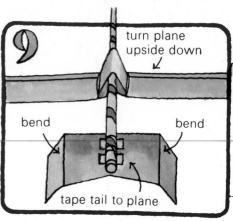

Put glue on the curved edge of the wing formers. Glue them on to the wings along the lines you drew each side of the notch.

Cut out a piece of card 5 cm × 3·25 cm. Glue its long edges to the bottom edges of the wing formers so that the wings become angled like this.

Slit the end of a straw (a). Twist the slit end into a point, push it into another straw to make one long straw (b). Tape the middle of this long straw into the cockpit (c).

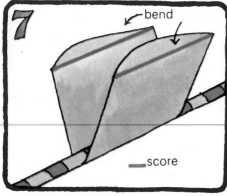

Score the cockpit along the lines you traced. Bend the cockpit along the score lines as shown.

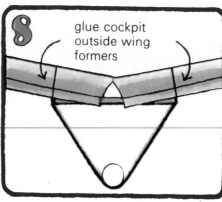

Glue together the wings and cockpit with the cockpit outside the wing formers as shown.

Put the plane upside down and tape the tail on to it like this with the straw lying along the line down the middle of the tail. Bend the sides of the tail as shown.

3

a

tape
half stuck
on to wing

pencil rolled up
to end of notch

b

tape stuck over edge

c

Half stick some tape along the notched edge of one wing as shown (a). Then put a ROUND pencil on to the unstuck half of the tape in line with the front wing edge.

Roll the pencil up the wing as far as the end of the notch (b). Then unroll the pencil and take the tape off it very carefully. Do it again on the other wing.

Fold the free edge of the tape up over the wing edge like this (c). The curve you have just made is called a camber.

The Drinking Straw Glider

silver-foil
or plasticine

Put enough weight on the front of the nose to make it fly in a smooth glide. Use silver foil or plasticine.

Pre-Flight Check

wings at same angle

tail flat

The Glider should look like this from the front. The tail must be flat and the wings must be at the same angle.

Jungle Fighter KH20

Make the Jungle Fighter KH20
difficult to spot by camouflaging it.
See page 9 on making
a tracing.
You will need
THE PATTERN FROM
   PAGE 29
card from a document folder
a sheet of paper
a large cardboard box
a large sheet of stiff paper
a small bit of thick card
tracing paper and a pencil
scissors and strong glue
sticky tape and a ruler
a ball point pen for scoring
Magic Markers for camouflage

Jungle Fighters

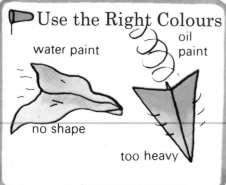

Do not use water-based paints on
the planes. The paper will crumple
up and lose its shape. Oil paints
are too heavy. Colour them with
Magic Markers.

Put a large cardboard box on its
side. Cut off the top side. Cut
out a curved shape from the extra
cardboard as shown. Tape the
shape on to the back of the box.

Make a roof by laying some stiff
paper over the curved shape and
taping it to the sides of the box.
Camouflage it by painting it the
same colour as its surroundings.

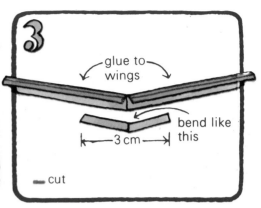

Trace and cut out a card cockpit and cockpit top. Score and bend the cockpit top as shown and glue it into the top of the cockpit.

Trace and cut out a paper nose (a). Bend the nose piece round, dab glue on its tab and join it up (b). Glue it to the front of the cockpit (c).

Trace and cut out its paper wings. Make a small snip as shown and camber them (page 14). Cut out a narrow strip of thick card. Bend it, glue the wings on to it as shown.

Put the wings on top of the cockpit. Bend the front and back cockpit top tabs over the wings and tape as shown.

Trace and cut out a paper fuselage. Bend it as shown. Put glue on its tab and glue it together (a). Trace and cut out a paper tail. Bend the tail sides up where shown.

Glue the fuselage into the back of the cockpit like this. Glue the tail on top of the end of the fuselage as shown (b).

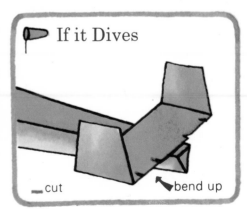

Put a strip of sticky tape over the front of the cockpit. Trace and cut out a card cockpit back. Score it and glue it into the back of the cockpit.

If it stalls it means that the nose is not heavy enough. Make the nose heavier by squeezing plasticine into it or crunching silver foil around it.

If it dives, it means that the nose is too heavy. Take some weight off the nose or make tail elevators (page 5). Bend them up as shown.

The Hawkeye Devastator

The Hawkeye Devastator flies out of doors. Launch it against the wind. Its propeller spins round when it flies. See page 9 on making a tracing.

You will need

THE PATTERN ON PAGES 30 AND 31
card from a document folder
a big sheet of paper
tracing paper and a pencil
a rubber band and a straw
a 3cm long big-headed pin
2 ball point pens
scissors and a ruler
sticky tape and glue
a needle and thread

Trace and cut out a paper fuselage, a paper fuselage top and two card stiffeners. Score the fuselage as shown.

Bend the fuselage sides up along the score lines. Glue stiffener (a) and (b) into the fuselage as shown. Stiffener (b) should touch the bottom edge of stiffener (a).

The Hawkeye Devastator

3 glue on fuselage top

trim any overlap

Bend the fuselage tabs in and glue the fuselage top on to the fuselage like this. When the glue is dry, trim off any overlapping paper.

4 bend

bend

score

Trace and cut out two card cockpit pieces. Score them both like this. Bend the bottom cockpit tabs up so that they lie flat on a table.

5 stiffener

fuselage and cockpit pieces level

glue on cockpit pieces

Glue the cockpit pieces on to the sides of the fuselage. Do this on a flat surface so that the bottom edge of each cockpit is in a straight line with the fuselage.

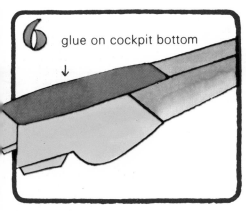

6 glue on cockpit bottom

Trace and cut out a card cockpit bottom. Turn the fuselage over. Put glue on the tabs at the bottom of the cockpit and glue the cockpit bottom on as shown.

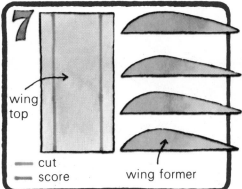

7 wing top

cut
score

wing former

Trace and cut out a card wing top and four card wing formers. You must trace the score and cut lines on the wing top. Then score and cut it like this.

8 glue

glue

glue

glue

Put glue on to the curved edges of two of the wing formers. Glue them to the wing top along the score and partly cut lines as shown.

9 underside of wings

wing strut mark

tape   wing strut mark

Trace and cut out two card wings. Remember to trace the wing strut marks. Put sticky tape on the straight edge of each wing as shown.

10 underside of wing

use two pencils

Camber each wing (page 14). You will have to use TWO round pencils instead of one. Make sure that they touch each other. Roll them both forward at the same speed.

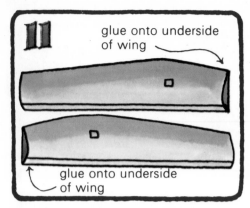

11 glue onto underside of wing

glue onto underside of wing

Put glue on to the curved edges of the other two wing formers and glue them on to the wings so that they look like this.

12 glue wings to wing top

glue here

glue here

wings and wing top in straight line

Glue the wing formered edges of the wings under the wing top flaps as shown. Make sure that the front edges of the wings and wing top lie in a straight line.

13 slot cockpit pieces into gap between wing formers

glue inside

Put glue on the inside of the curves at the top of the cockpit pieces and slip them up into the wing top so that each piece slots between two wing formers.

17 a

fold struts over and glue

b

c

score

strut tabs

Trace and cut out two card struts. Score each one as shown (a). Fold each one down the middle score line and glue (b). Bend along the other score lines as shown. (c).

18 glue to strut mark

glue

plane upside down

Turn the plane upside down. Glue one of the strut tabs on to the wings over the wing strut mark. Do the same with the other strut on the other wing.

19 wings must tilt up at same angle

glue struts under fuselage

Turn the plane over. Move the free end of each strut tab up and down the fuselage base until both wings are at the same angle. Then glue the strut tabs on to the base.

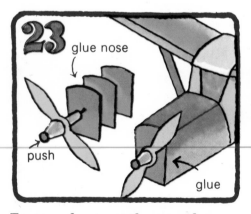

23 glue nose

push

glue

Trace and cut out three card noses. Glue them together. Push the long propeller pin firmly through them as shown. Glue them into the nose like this.

24 glue nose top on

Bend the tabs at the front of the cockpit pieces inwards. Trace and cut out a paper nose top. Glue it round the front of the cockpit.

25 plane top

Trace and cut out a paper plane top. Put glue on to it and glue it over the middle of the wings so that it hides the score and cut marks on the wing top.

14 bend tail tabs flat

Bend the tail tabs at the end of the fuselage down on to each other so that they form a flat and level surface on which to glue the tail.

15 glue onto tabs — trace middle line

Trace the tail and the line going across it on to card. Cut it out. Put glue on the tail tabs and glue the tail on to them with the line going exactly down the middle.

16 glue tail fin over middle line

Trace and cut out a card tail fin. Glue it down on to the middle line on the tail as shown.

20 make a hole — twist — cut

Trace and cut out a card propeller. Make a hole with a knitting needle where shown. Gently twist one blade in one direction and the other in the other direction.

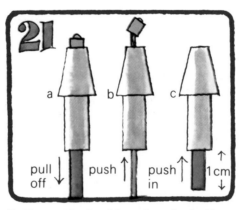

21 a b c — pull off — push — push in — 1 cm

Pull out the inside tube of a ball point pen (a). Push the ball point out of the bearing with a long pin (b). Cut 1 cm off the inside tube, push it back into the bearing (c).

22 tape — push pin

Push the bearing through the hole in the propeller as shown. Tape the propeller to the bearing. Push the long big-headed pin through the hole in the middle of the bearing.

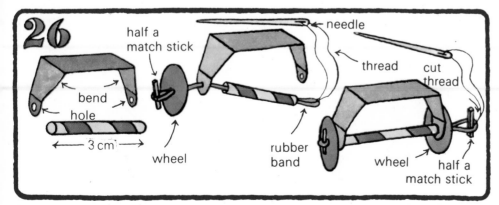

26 half a match stick — needle — thread — cut thread — bend — hole — 3 cm — wheel — rubber band — wheel — half a match stick

Trace and cut out two card wheels and a card undercarriage. Make holes where shown. Score the undercarriage and bend its sides. Cut a straw as shown. Push a needle, thread and rubber band through undercarriage, wheels and straw as shown. Stop the rubber band ends with half a match stick. Cut the thread.

27 glue to fuselage

Turn the plane upside down again. Glue the undercarriage on to the base of the cockpit just in front of the struts as shown.

Flying Tips

If you have managed to make your aeroplanes glide smoothly in a straight line, you might like to try making them fly in other ways. On this page you can find out how to make the different controls on an aeroplane that make it fly in different directions and perform flying tricks. Some of these, like looping-the-loop and S-bends take a lot of practice.

Making a Plane with a Keel turn left and right

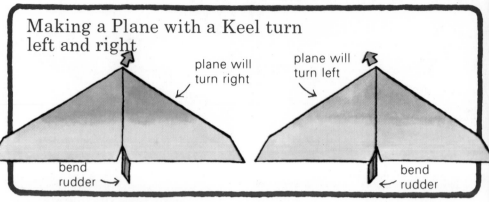

Planes with a keel like darts and Air Scorpions can be made to turn left and right by making a short snip through the keel just at the back under the wings and sticking the two sides together with tape. This is a rudder. Bend the rudder left to make the plane turn left, bend it right to make the plane turn right.

Making a Plane without a Keel turn left and right

To make these planes turn you can give their wings ailerons. Make two cuts on each wing as shown. To make a plane fly to the left, bend the left aileron up and bend the right aileron down. To make a plane fly to the right, bend the right aileron up and the left one down.

Planes with Tail Fins

If your plane has ailerons and a tail fin, bend the ailerons in the usual way and bend the end of the tail fin to point in the direction you want the plane to fly.

Turning by Launching

A plane set to fly straight can be made to fly left by launching it at this angle. Tilt it in the other direction to make it turn right. This is launching it in a bank.

S-Bends

If you find it easy to launch your plane in a bank, try making it do an S-Bend. Set the controls to make it fly one way then launch it in a bank in the opposite direction.

Looping-the-Loop

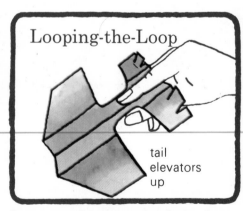

Some people can make their planes loop-the-loop. Bend the tail elevators up, point the plane down and launch it very hard. This takes a lot of practice.

Flying out-of-Doors

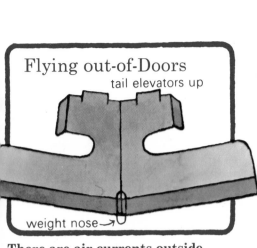

tail elevators up

weight nose →

There are air currents outside which make it more difficult for a paper plane to fly. Try making your plane heavier by weighting the nose. Bend the elevators up.

1 Flying in a Wind

Aeroplanes can do strange things in a wind. If you launch a plane so that it flies in the same direction as the wind, it will fly much faster than it would inside.

2

If you launch a plane in the opposite direction to the way the wind is blowing, it may fly backwards like this.

If you want, you can make an obstacle course by tying brooms to chairs and flying your planes through and round them.

Fling Gliding

Heavier planes can be exciting to fly by fling gliding. Tie one end of a piece of string to the edge of a wing, tie the other end to a strong stick or ruler. Bend the tail elevators up a bit. Hold the stick and turn round and round facing the stick all the time. See how long you can make the string without losing control.

Air Race

This is a game to test your skill at flying paper planes. Any number of players can play it. Everybody will need a paper plane and a counter. What you do is to make yourselves an aerobatics course like the one on page 23. You fly your plane on the course and then you move your counter along the board. The number of spaces you move your counter depends on how you fly your plane. Each flying trick is worth a different number of points. If you fly your plane to the left, it is worth 2 points, so you move your counter on 2 spaces on the board. Have a look at the score board and see what each trick is worth. Fly your planes in turn. When your counter lands on a space, you have to do what it says on the box. Try not to let your counter land on the hazard boxes. The player whose counter gets to the airport at the end of the course first is the winner. If you want, you can play the game with dice and counters only.

SCORE BOARD

S BEND	6
RIGHT TURN	3
LEFT TURN	2
FLYING STRAIGHT	1
CRASHING	0
DIVING	0
SPINNING	0
STALLING	0

7 STEADY FLYING

8 FORGOT SANDWICHES GO BACK TO BASE

6 STEADY FLYING

15 FIRE IN ENGINE GO BACK TO 12

5 ENGINE TROUBLE GO BACK TO 2

16 STEADY FLYING

4 STEADY FLYING

23 HIJACKED GO BACK TO 16

3 STEADY FLYING

24 COLLISION COURSE MISS A TURN

2 STEADY FLYING

31 AIR POCKET GO BACK TO 25

1 DELAYED BY FOG MISS A TURN

32 STEADY FLYING

START

Hang Gliders

One of the first aeroplanes was a Hang Glider. It was invented by a German called Otto Lilienthal in 1891. He was a very successful pioneer of flying. He had no controls on his glider. He hung by his arms under it and changed its direction by swinging his body.

You will need
a polythene bag at least
   20 × 20cm
4 drinking straws
a small, light, plastic figure
   or plasticine and a paper clip
scissors, thread and sticky tape

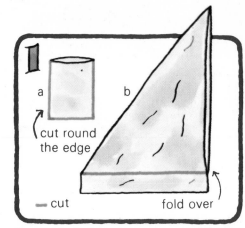

Cut round the edges of a polythene bag (a). Fold one piece as shown to make a square (b).

Tape two straws along the edge of the polythene as shown. Turn it over and tape the straws on from the other side too.

The Hang Glider

3

a

fold polythene in half

— cut

b

push straw inside with end sticking out

c

unfold and tape straw to polythene

Fold in half and snip 1 cm off its front (a). Push another straw inside the polythene with its end sticking out at the front (b).

Unfold very gently. Try to keep the third straw exactly in the middle. Then tape it on to the polythene as shown (c).

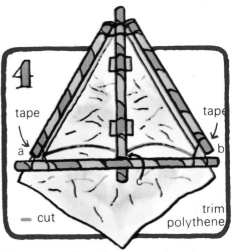

4

tape

tape

a

b

c

— cut

trim polythene

Tape on a fourth straw at corners (a) and (b) only. Trim off middle straw (c). Trim the polythene as shown.

5

tape to middle of back straw

Tape the middle straw to the fourth straw as shown. Your polythene should be a little baggy, and not taped at the back.

6

tape

Tie or tape a small, light plastic figure to the centre straw as shown to balance the plane. A plasticine weighted paper clip will balance the plane if you have no toy.

How Lilienthal changed his Glider's Direction

Lilienthal swung his body in different directions to make his glider fly differently. To raise the nose, he made the glider tail heavy by swinging his legs back.

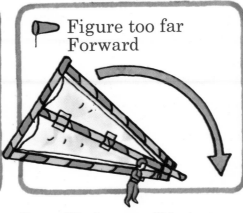

Figure too far Forward

Your glider's nose will be too heavy and the glider will dive. Move the figure back until your Hang Glider flies smoothly.

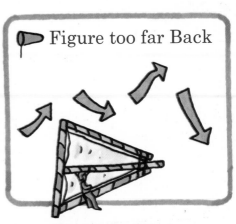

Figure too far Back

Your glider's tail will be too heavy and the glider will stall. Move the figure forward bit by bit until the plane glides smoothly.

27

Patterns for Tracing

Air
Scorpion
Tail Fin

fold

Moon Bug

Range Moth

fold

Range Moth
Tail Fin

fold

Key

trace this line as well

place on fold

Trace on to paper

trace on to card

fold

Moon Bug
Tail Fin

fold

fold

Trace straight lines with
a ruler.

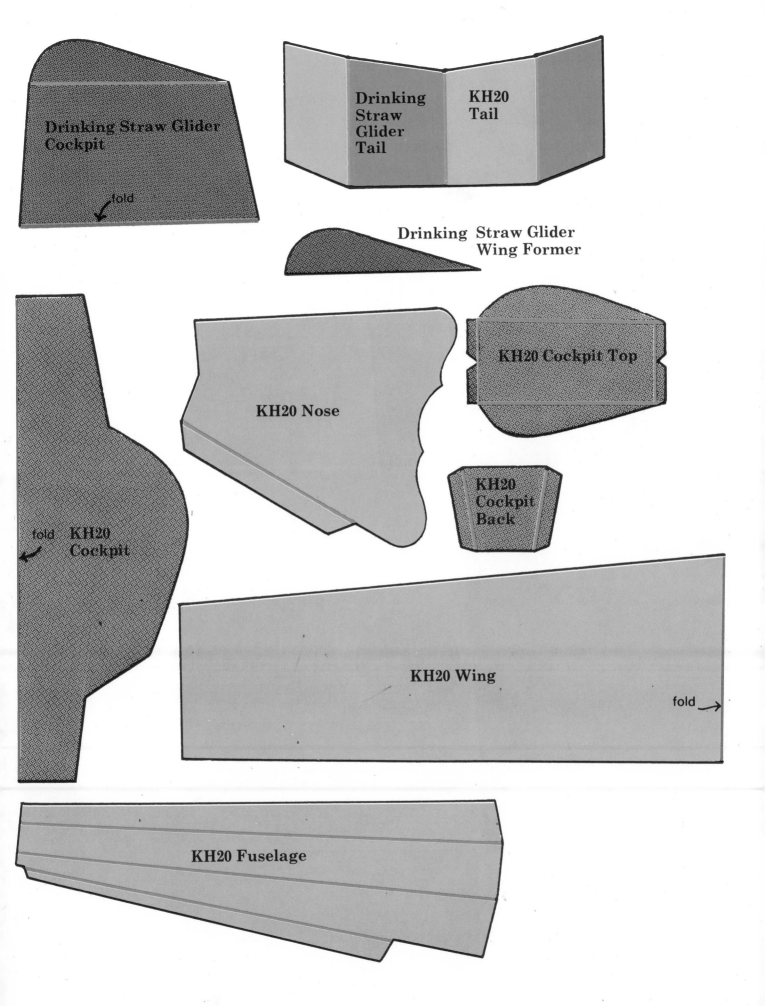

Drinking Straw Glider Cockpit

fold

Drinking Straw Glider Tail

KH20 Tail

Drinking Straw Glider Wing Former

KH20 Nose

KH20 Cockpit Top

KH20 Cockpit Back

fold KH20 Cockpit

KH20 Wing

fold

KH20 Fuselage

Patterns for Tracing
Hawkeye Devastator

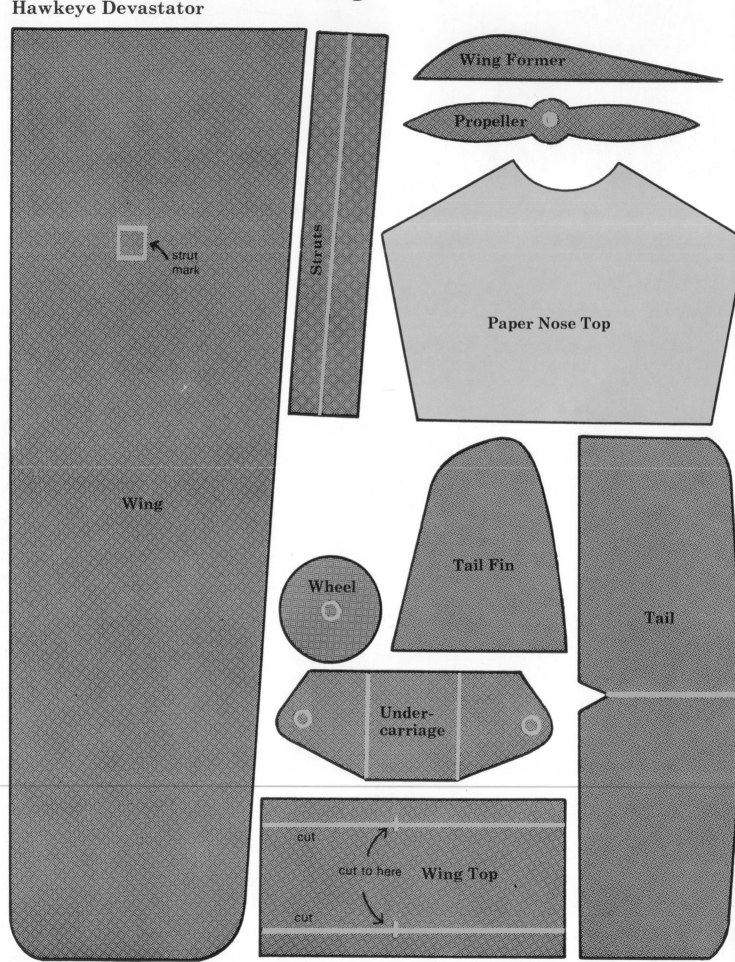

Wing Former

Propeller

Paper Nose Top

Struts

strut mark

Wing

Wheel

Tail Fin

Tail

Under-carriage

cut

cut to here

cut

Wing Top

Fuselage Top

Plane Top

Nose

Cockpit

Cockpit Bottom

Stiffener a

Fuselage

Stiffener b

Going Further

Microfilm Model

This model is made of balsa wood covered with very thin microfilm, It flies indoors and only weighs one gramme.

Simple Gliders for you to Make

If you want to try making a plane from balsa wood, you should start with a simple balsa glider which you can buy quite cheaply.

Where to Shop

If you look at the last pages of an aeromodelling magazine you will find a list of model shops. They are listed town by town so that you can go to the nearest one.

Finding out More

You should be able to find out more about model aeroplanes by writing to any of the following addresses:

Model Aeronautical Association of Australia, Hon. Sec. Gordon Burford, Witton Street, Flagstaff Hill 5179, South Australia.
Model Aeronautical Association of Canada, Box 9, Oakville, Ontario, Canada.
Model Aeronautics Council of Ireland, John McNally, Marieville, Bendermeer Park, Magazine Road, Cork.
Northern Ireland Association of Aeromodellers, Hon. Sec. Maurice Doyle, 28 Carlston Avenue, Holywood, Co. Down.
New Zealand Model Aeronautical Association, Hon. Sec. John Malkin, 51 Clyma Street, Upper Hutt.
Scottish Aeromodellers' Association, Hon. Sec. P. Malone, 105 Sighthill Loam, Edinburgh FH11 4NT.
South African Model Aeronautic Association, P.O. Box 4, Howard Place, Pinelands, Cape.
Society of Model Aeronautical Engineers, Dept MS, 116 Pall Mall, London SW1Y 5EB.

Books about Planes

How to Make and Fly Paper Aircraft	Captain Ralph S Barnaby	(Piccolo 1973)
Jet-Age Jamboree	Yasuaki Ninomiya	(Japan Publications Inc. 1968)
Aircraft	K. Munson	(MacDonald Visual Book 1971)
Aeromodeller Annuals		(Model & Allied Publications 1948)
Aeromodeller Pocket Data Book	P. G. F. Chinn	(Model & Allied Publications 1968)
Model Plane Building from A—Z	Flying Models Staff	(Carstens Publications U.S.A. 1969)
A Beginner's Guide to Building and Flying Model Aircraft	Robert Lopshire	(Harper & Row 1967)
Model Airplane Handbook	Howard McEntee	(Thomas Y Crowell U.S.A.)
Control-Line Manual	R. G. Moulton	(Model & Allied Publications 1973)
The World of Model Aircraft	Guy R Williams	(Andre Deutsch 1973)

Magazines about Planes

Aero	46, Porter Street, Prahan, Victoria 3181, Australia.
Aero Modeller	P.O. Box 35, Bridge St., Hemel Hempstead, Herts, England.
Airborne	P.O. Box 205, Blacktown 2148, Australia.
Free Flight News	11, Parkside Rd., Sunningdale, Ascot, Berks SL5 0NL, England.
Model Aeroplane Gazette	12, Slayleigh Ave., Sheffield, England.
NON News of the North	R. Magill, 1852 Great North Rd., Auckland 7, New Zealand.
Radio Modeller	64, Wellington Rd., Hampton Hill, Mddx. England.
Wings	113, Winchester House, Loveday St., Johannesburg, S. Africa.